Saving Water

Contents | Page

written by John Lockyer

Red Rocket Readers™
Engineered by Flying Start Books

We love water! We drink it. We cook with it. It keeps us clean. We can put water on plants in the garden, too.

Water is fun. We can play and swim in it. On a hot day, it is cool to get wet.

There is a lot of water on the planet. Most of it is in the seas. We do not drink sea water. We drink fresh water. We cook and clean with it, too. Most fresh water comes from rain, rivers, and lakes.

ocean

A dam is put across a river to block the water. This water spreads into a big lake.

Pipes bring the water to our homes. When we need it, we can turn the water on and off.

In very dry places, humans need more water than they can get. They have many ways to save water.

They dig deep pits to catch the rain.
If they find water underground,
they can dig a well.

We can save water, too. Lots of water is lost from drips. Check your kitchen and bathrooms for drips.

dishwashing

A short shower is better than a bath. Turn off the water when you brush your teeth. Do not fill the sink when you clean the dishes.

You can save water in the garden, too. Catch rain water off the roof. A tank of rain water will fill a watering can many times. You can clean your bike, car, or pet with a bucket of water. This tip will save you lots of water.

watering can

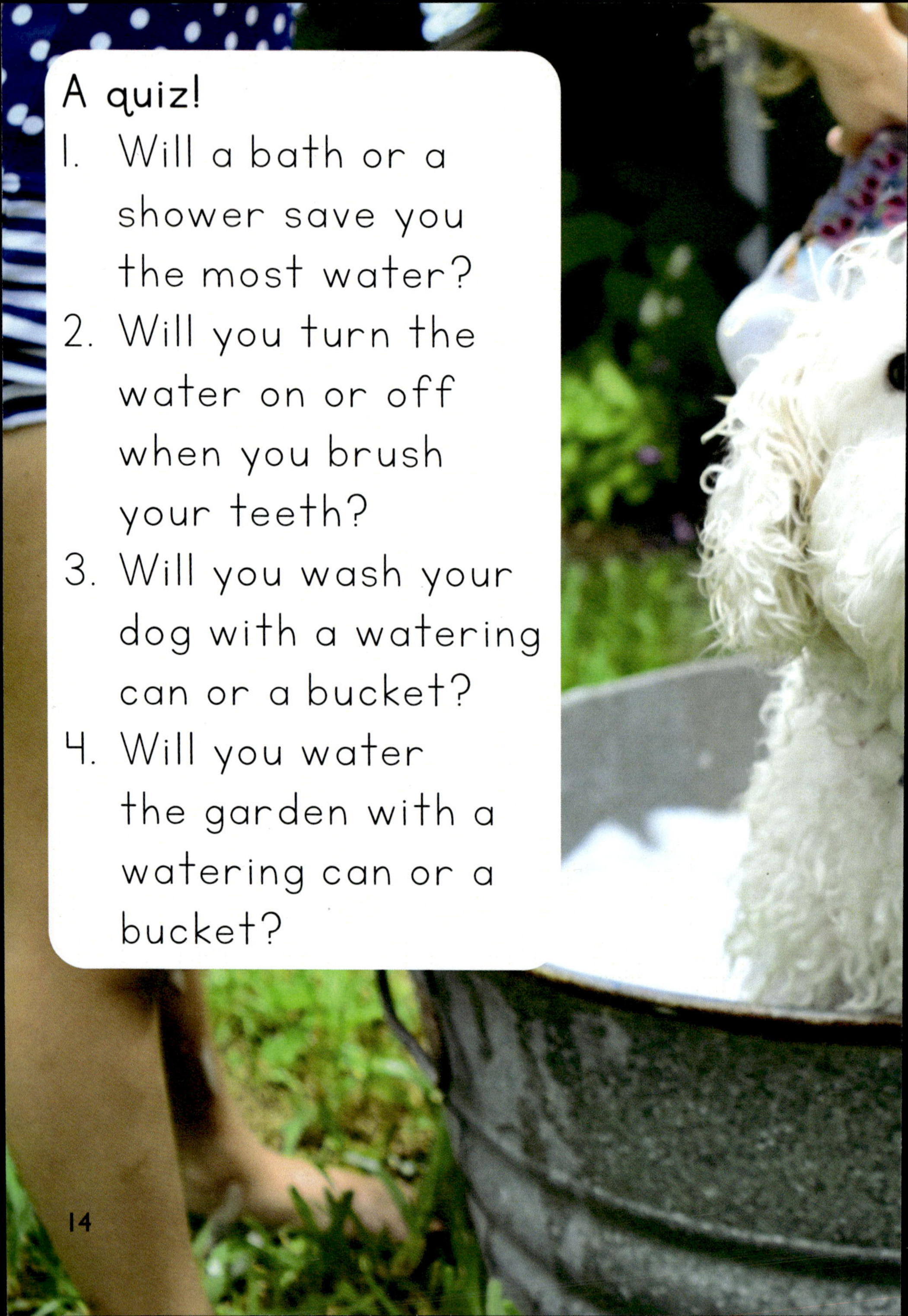

A quiz!

1. Will a bath or a shower save you the most water?
2. Will you turn the water on or off when you brush your teeth?
3. Will you wash your dog with a watering can or a bucket?
4. Will you water the garden with a watering can or a bucket?

dog bath

Think of more ways to save water!